ATTENTION

Category: Business & Economics

Description: Get attention with an irresistible offer. Every time you visit a customer you will know what to bring that will really help their business. It could be a very special price on an item, a piece of industry news, an idea that will help their business, something that will give them a competitive advantage, or perhaps something personal that you know they are interested in. You will learn how to make them look forward to your visit. Benjamin Franklin's 13-week self improvement program will guarantee your success.

Copyright Bob Oros-2017
ISBN 978-1-105-22290-0

Written and published by Bob Oros

ATTENTION: 1

Attention Get attention with irresistible compelling offers 6

Set the Stage 7

Gone in 60 seconds 10

The first minute 12

Making a cold call? 14

How often are your customers interrupted 17

I was in the neighborhood… 19

The first 60 seconds 29

Resisting new ideas 31

POS material 35

Using samples 36

A small gift 36

Industry news 37

Your mental picture 41

Create demand 44

My 4% improvement objective: 51

What the entire book series will do for you 53

Ben Franklin's system 54

Achieve a 52% improvement 59

Attention

Get attention with irresistible offers

Set the Stage

This short article from the Washington Post was sent to me by a friend, John Boylan, VP Sales and Marketing for Berks Foods.

The story reminded me of one of the most important points to remember when selling your products and services. Read on and I'm sure you will agree...

THE SITUATION

In Washington, DC, at a Metro Station, on a cold January morning, this man with a violin played six Bach pieces for about 45 minutes. During that time, approximately 2,000 people went through the station, most of them on their way to work. After about 3 minutes, a middle-aged man noticed that there was a musician playing. He slowed his pace and stopped for a few seconds, and then he hurried on to meet his schedule.

About 4 minutes later:

The violinist received his first dollar. A woman threw money in the hat and, without stopping, continued to walk.

At 6 minutes:

A young man leaned against the wall to listen to him, then looked at his watch and started to walk again.

At 10 minutes:

A 3-year old boy stopped, but his mother tugged him along hurriedly. The kid stopped to look at the violinist again, but the mother pushed hard and the child continued to walk, turning his head the whole time. This action was repeated by several other children, but every parent - without exception - forced their children to move on quickly.

At 45 minutes:

The musician played continuously. Only 6 people stopped and listened for a short while. About 20 gave money but continued to walk at their normal pace. The man collected a total of $32.

After 1 hour:

He finished playing and silence took over. No one noticed and no one applauded. There was no recognition at all.

No one knew this, but the violinist was Joshua Bell, one of the greatest musicians in the world. He played one of the most intricate pieces ever written, with a violin worth $3.5 million dollars. Two days before, Joshua Bell sold-out a theater in Boston where the seats averaged $100 each to sit and listen to him play the same music.

This is a true story. Joshua Bell, playing incognito in the D.C Metro Station, was organized by the Washington Post as part of a social experiment about perception, taste and people's priorities. The lesson this so clearly demonstrates is the importance of setting the stage when you make a sale. It points out the necessity of positioning your product in a way that even if it is a commodity, when surrounded by a stage of quality, service and a great company reputation, the value goes up, and so does the price. It also points out that the product is a very small part of the total sales process.

This is what it means to sell the sizzle, not the steak. In copywriting this is called "theater." You make your point by surrounding it with a story. I use "theater" in just about every email I send out, including this one. And if you have read this far, you can see how well it works.

Gone in 60 seconds

Ours is a fast paced society, a society on the move. Information overload has set in. Thousands of ad agencies, politicians, entertainment media, and many others are competing for our scarce time as well as the scarce time of our customers. By necessity and out of habit, the attention span has shrunk. We want the news of the world in a half hour or less. The quicker the better.

The same goes for entertainment. Remember when you felt "ripped off" if a movie was less than two hours long? Few of them were. Today, we get bored if a film is over two hours. Thirty second and even fifteen second "important messages" are used today instead of one-minute advertisements.

This overwhelming intrusion aimed at us day in and day out has deadened our senses. We can no longer assume that we have our customer's attention when we attempt to communicate with them. The quantity of information aimed at customers has caused them to block out messages more than ever. Customers are time constrained, barely able to keep up with their present concerns. When confronted with your new selling message most customers simply don't care.

Is it any wonder that 90% of sales are lost in the first minute of the sales call?

What can we do or say to make our sales call more effective? Every time we call on one of our accounts to present a new product or service, or even to simply get an order, there is a preliminary process we must go through or we will lose before we even begin. We must have their full attention, or we will fall into the category of the 90 percent who lose the sale in the first minute.

The first minute

What you do or say in that first minute of your sales presentation is more important than any other step in the sale.

A = Attention. You first must get the prospects attention with a strong statement or headline.

I = Interest. Once you have their attention you must convert it to interest. This is where you use a powerful testimonial or some relevant facts that will impact their business.

D = Details or Desire. In a sales presentation or sales letter this is where you give the details of what you are selling with the goal of arousing a desire in the prospects mind strong enough to make them want to have what you are selling.

A = Action. Here is the point that you ask them to buy.

Another way to look at this first minute is the 3 - 3 - 30 system.

You have 3 seconds to get their attention, 3 seconds to establish relevancy and 30 seconds to tell your story.

Turn and point to any person within range of your vision right now. That individual is dominated for the time being with a particular ATTITUDE. This attitude is controlling their entire personality. It is coloring their mental and emotional life. They see you through this attitude. Anything you say to them must be sifted through the screen of this fixed ATTITUDE before you can get a spark of interest in what you are talking about.

I don't think I exaggerate when I say that ninety percent of the sales you lose are mishandled in the first crucial moment. When you or I face the prospect ready to speak our first sentence we find ourselves squarely up against an attitude as closed as a barn door. What we do or say in that first sentence is more important than any other step in the sale . . . because we can't possibly sell a person who continues to retain the attitude they had before we came in.

What can we do on every call which will swing the prospects attitude so they will listen with interest to what we have to say? It's this original attitude which licks more conscientious, hard-working salespeople than all of the objections in the book.

You must have an opener which breaks through that attitude and provoke the prospect to say, "Sure, I'll listen to what you have to say with an open mind. Come on in and tell your story."

What is your most successful opener? What line have you used to open your prospects mind and have them lean forward and ask for more?

Making a cold call?

Most people sense that cold calls are self-serving to the person calling. After all, when someone makes a cold call it is because they want something. Otherwise why would you be calling!

For cold calling to be done in a non-intrusive way, we must shift the perception away from "I want something from you," into "I am being helpful." When our cold calls do not feel intrusive, people naturally are more open to talking with us.

To be perceived as helpful, we must actually be helpful. If we are sincere in our approach and desire to help the other person much of the resistance will fade away.

Here's how to start being helpful:

1. Make It About Them, Not About You. We've all been taught that selling is to talk and present. However, this self-focus almost always feels intrusive to the customer and shuts down the possibility of a genuine conversation.

Instead, step directly into their situation. Our job is to ask questions and listen. Simple question that will get the conversation going. They are sometimes referred to as Grants tomb questions - "Who's buried in Grant's tomb?"

2. Avoid the Artificial Enthusiasm. People feel pushed along by artificial enthusiasm. This triggers rejection because it feels very intrusive to be pushed by someone they don't know. Artificial enthusiasm includes some expectation that our product or service is a great fit for them. Yet, we've never spoken with them before, much less had a full conversation with them. We can't possibly know much about them or their needs. It is better to modestly assume you know very little about them. Invite them to share with you some of their concerns and difficulties. And allow them to guide the conversation, even when it means getting "off track" a bit.

3. Focus on One Compelling Problem to Solve. Don't go into a pitch the way you would if you were operating out of the traditional sales mindset. Make what you say about them, not about you. Try to keep in mind that who you are and what you have to offer are irrelevant at this

moment. The key is to identify a problem that you believe the other person might have. Address one specific, concrete problem that you know most businesses experience. Don't make any mention of you or any solutions you have to offer.

4. Consider "Where Should We Go from Here?" Let's say the initial call turns into a positive and friendly conversation. The other person feels you're offering something valuable and wants to know more. Both of you feel there may be a reason for another meeting. Rather than focusing on making a sale at this point, you can simply say, "Well, where do you think we should go from here?" This question reassures potential clients that you're not using the conversation to fulfill your own hidden agenda. Rather, your giving them space and time to come to their own conclusions. You're helping them create the direction they want to go, and you will follow.

It is always a personal challenge to walk into a strangers business and try to make a friend. However, Course, that's what it's all about.

How often are your customers interrupted?

In addition to being constantly interrupted by someone trying to sell something or a business problem every eight minutes, our customers are also affected by their attitude.

Turn and point to any person within range of your vision right now. That individual is dominated for the time being with a particular ATTITUDE. This attitude is controlling their entire personality. They see you through this attitude. Anything you say to them must be sifted through the screen of this fixed ATTITUDE before you can get a spark of interest in what you are talking about. When you or I face the prospect ready to speak our first sentence we find ourselves squarely up against an attitude as closed as a barn door. What we do or say in that first sentence is more important than any other step in the sale . . . because we can't possibly sell a person who continues to retain the attitude they had before we came in.

What can we do on every call which will swing the prospects attitude so they will listen with interest to what we have to say? It's this original attitude which licks more conscientious, hard-working salespeople than all of the objections in the book. You'd give a week's salary to find one opener which would break through that attitude and provoke the prospect to say, "Sure, I'll listen to what you have to say with an open mind. Come on in and tell me more."

I was in the neighborhood…

Sometimes you have to take a negative approach to get a positive response, sometimes you have to be creative to get someone's attention in the first place, and sometimes you have to really think outside the box to make people take notice.

I am going to give you an example that is going to blow your mind. But first, let me show you a couple of things I have in my files that really seem to work, and some that don't.

Whenever I am on an airplane or in a crowd of strangers I am asked what I do. According to the experts you should have an "elevator speech" for these occasions. You should be able to tell people what you do by the time the elevator makes it from one floor to the next.

I designed a clever 30 second speech and it really seemed to turn people off. As soon as I said I was a "sales trainer" I could see the expression on their face turn to panic. They immediately said they don't use sales trainers, or they have a company employee who does their sales training. They had a ready-made objection. So by following the advice of the experts, I was turning people off in less than 30 seconds.

Back to the drawing board. I took a different approach by thinking outside the box.

I created a "shock" effect and I am now able to get people's interest and have some fun at the same time. Now, when they ask me what I do, here is what I say:

"I show people how to stay 4 steps ahead of the sheriff, would you like to know what those 4 steps are?" And they always say YES?

I give them four quick steps that would be applicable to them and ask which step would be most helpful. If they say "step 3" I give them a good sound bite of information on step 3. I then get their business card and follow up with some more helpful information.

I am getting ready to do a 5,000-piece mailing and guess what will be on the envelope? You got it: "How to stay 4 steps ahead of the sheriff, would you like to know what the 4 steps are?"

When you are approaching a new account think of your first few words as the sales copy on the envelope. The job of the sales copy is NOT to make the sale, but to get them to OPEN IT UP!

Keep in mind that if they don't open the envelope the sale will NEVER be made! The same with your opening line. If you don't hit the right button the door doesn't open.

Here are some of the standard openers and my translation. If you are guilty you might spend a little time creating something that works for you. Be easy on yourself, everyone has used them.

"I am sorry for interrupting."

Translation: I really don't amount to much - you are much more important than I am - you see I am just a doormat waiting for someone to wipe their feet on me.

"I know you are busy."

Translation: I really don't have any respect for you or your time - you are a busy and important person and I am intruding in you day.

"I was in the neighborhood."

Translation: I am not very organized - I simply drift through my day from neighborhood to neighborhood making random calls on people and waste their time.

"Do you need anything?"

Translation. I am really not much of a salesperson and I was wondering if there are any crumbs left over from a real sales person who has been here.

"I wanted to stop by and introduce myself."

Translation. I am really not ambitious enough to have done some homework about you so I guess I will tell you all about ME.

I think you get the point. Things are different out there today, so you must be different or they eat you alive.

Today's customers are being bombarded with an estimated 3,000 sales and marketing messages every day. How do you stand out and set yourself apart from the crowd? You have to hit them with a HUGE

BENEFIT. A benefit that will have the same power as if you hit them between the eyes with a baseball bat!

How should you make your entrance into an account?

First: Attitude. You should always assume an attitude of confidence and purpose. Never apologize for making the call. Never feel like you are interrupting. Never say, "I was in the neighborhood" as if your call was not important. Never say, "I wanted to stop by and introduce myself." Who cares?

There is a psychological law that makes the prospect react and respond to the attitude and action expressed by you the salesperson. There is nothing complicated about it, except the results that come when you put this psychological law into effect. Make the call with confidence.

Second. A huge SPECIFIC BENEFIT. For example.: "I am here to show you how you can lower your operating expenses by $5,323 dollars per quarter -or- I am here to show you how increase your invoice size by 25 cents, which equates to $813 per week, let me show you how I figured it based on your current volume -or- I have a product that will cut your cleaning time by 23% resulting in a labor cost savings of $103 per week or $5,356 per year."

I can hear you now. "But Bob, I have to call on my customers every week!" How could I possibly come up with a new money saving or money-making idea for my customers EVERY WEEK?"

My answer. How many items do you have? 2,000? 4,000? 8,000? 10,000? Every item you have in your inventory represents an opportunity. How many services do you have? 27? 37? 47? Or how about 57?

I can still hear you. "But Bob, all my competitors are selling on price and I have to meet their prices or lose the business."

What if your competitor was giving their product away FREE? What if there was very little quality difference between your product and the "free" product? What if their method of distribution was much more efficient than yours? Could you sell against that kind of competition? No?

Well someone was given a sales challenge to sell against that kind of market condition. And they are very successful. The product is bottled water. How do they do it? Do they lower their price and try to compete with tap water? Do they badmouth the water company and tell their customers "yea, it may be free, but look at what you get!"

Is bottled water really any better? I gave it the ultimate taste test. I put two bowls of water in front of my dog – one from a bottle that I paid over a dollar for – the other from the sink faucet. My dog tried both of them. Which one do you think she preferred? The tap water! Did I switch to tap water? No. I still pay an outrageous price for a bottle of water.

Why? Somehow the perceived value of water in a bottle is a strong enough benefit for me to fork over my hard-earned cash.

Every item you sell has within it a huge benefit to the customer or you wouldn't be selling it. All you have to do is find ONE BENEFIT PER WEEK and present it to all your prospects.

Let's do the math. Five benefit presentations per day x one benefit per week x 52 weeks = 1,250 benefit presentations per year x 20% will give you 250 sales.

Even a blind hog can find an acorn once in a while. If you make ONE THOUSAND TWO HUNDRED AND FIFTY benefit presentations per year – you will sell something – even if by accident.

The bottom line. You walk into your account. There have been 2,999 people trying to sell this person today and you are number 3,000.

Do you say – "I'm sorry for interrupting?"

Do you say – "I know you are busy?"

Do you say – "I was in the neighborhood?"

Do you say – "Do you need anything?"

Do you say – "I wanted to stop by and introduce myself?"

Only if you want the customer to say – "Who cares?"

Benjamin Franklin drives home the point when he said: "Make yourselves sheep and the wolves will eat you."

Now for the one that is going to blow your mind!

Craig Gross, a friend of mine from Florida and a really good sales person went way outside the box to get his customer's attention. Let's have Craig tell it in his own words. Here is the email I received:

"I am waiting for one of my customers - so I thought with the few minutes I have I would send you a success story."

"At one of your seminars a few years back I remember you said something to the affect that when making a sales call you need to sometimes go way outside of the box to make an impression. Well, I do some ventriloquism on the side and the other day I got this hair brained idea that I would go into a prospect account with "Kenny" my vent puppet. The customer was caught so off balance and we had such a good laugh he told me to please come back."

"I certainly do not mind you telling my "ride with" story. Kenny is a big hit wherever I take him. I taught myself ventriloquism after doing puppet shows in children's church for several years. I just got this desire to learn how to "vent" and then my best friend from high school sent me a vent puppet that he had made - for free! People actually pay me now to do ventriloquist shows - I can't believe it."

Way to go Craig... a good example for all of us.

The first 60 seconds

When we see that our customers are busy, we should never apologize for interrupting. There is a psychological law that makes a customer react and respond to the attitude and action expressed by the salesperson, in the same manner. There is nothing mysterious about it, except the amazing results that come when you begin to put this law into effect. It makes sense. Everyone wants to do the appropriate thing. Everyone wants to "rise to the occasion." We act out our parts in accordance with the stage that we find set before us. There is an unconscious urge for the customer to "live up to" the expectations the salesperson has of them. You, the seller, have the power to set the stage. If you want your customer to be agreeable, act agreeable. Don't fall into the trap of responding to their actions and attitudes.

If you decide beforehand that a certain customer is going to be difficult to deal with, chances are you will approach them in a negative attitude, with your fists mentally clenched ready to fight. When you do this, you literally set the stage for them to act on. He or she rises to the occasion. The customer will act the part that you have set for them to act and you come away convinced that they really are a "tough customer," without ever realizing that your own actions and attitudes helped make them one.

In dealing with our customers, we see our own attitudes reflected to us in their behavior. When you smile, the person in front of you smiles. When you frown, the person frowns. When you shout, the person shouts back. A "Cutting Edge" salesperson realizes just how important and how predictable this law of psychology is.

Resisting new ideas

Customers resist the best ideas even after you have their full attention. The resistance starts with a negative feeling about the product, service or program. He or she hasn't investigated it yet. The immediate resistance is general. First, there's the risk. What if the idea doesn't pay off or the product doesn't perform?

Also, something new means change. And maybe the change will be uncomfortable. It will cause trouble, and who needs trouble?

This makes the prospect feel that they don't want to hear about what you are trying to sell. Even if you get them to listen, their generalized resistance adds strength to the objection.

Your customer will be on the defensive before you even begin to sell. It is in a person's nature to fear making a change that will cost money. During a sales presentation, your customer will almost always respond negatively to your pricing. It is part of their strategy to get you to lower your price.

By knowing what to expect you avoid giving in without making a case for your product. Salespeople frequently make the mistake of offering discounts up front in order to head off a potentially negative discussion about price.

A sales manager I worked for insisted that I call on a certain account every week even though it seemed hopeless to ever sell them. On the very first call the customer tore my business card up in little pieces. The customer had a problem with a previous salesperson. The salesperson had left the company with a grudge and had left several things undone. This customer had several special orders for a banquet. The day the product was due for delivery the customer found out that the salesperson had quit and never turned in the order. However, I followed orders and finally, after 37 weeks of calls, he gave in and bought something from me. If it had been up to me, I never would have done it, however, the boss followed up and asked me every week if I made the call.

Have the necessary persistence to overcome their resistance and plan to outlast the competition. You have the knowledge of knowing you can turn them into a customer if you stay with it.

Are you a person with vision or a short-range "whatever" person? Do you make things happen – or do you let things happen?

A person without vision must have instant gratification. They work on small goals that don't require too much effort. They are usually short on patience. If they can't have it now - they don't want it. A person without vision is always opening new accounts by making promises that are impossible to keep. A person without vision is TOUGH to work for.

On the other hand, a person with vision can plan into the future. They are able to look ahead and SEE the business they are going to have. They are always planting seeds today for tomorrow's business. They are not put off by hearing the word NO. A person with vision will do what they must do even if they don't FEEL like it. They know the best accounts are the ones that are hard to get.

And this is where persistence comes in.

PERSISTENCE - The number one quality of a person with vision. There are success stories that are simply unbelievable when you hear about the length of time it has taken a person with vision to land an account. This quality of PERSISTENCE is of vital importance in sales.

"Nothing in the world can take the place of persistence. Talent will not; there is nothing more commonplace than unsuccessful people with talent. Genius will not;

unrewarded genius is almost a proverb. Education alone will not; the world is full of educated derelicts. Persistence and Determination alone are omnipotent. " Earl Nightingale.

Do you have persistence? Take the test to see how much persistence you have. Ask yourself this one question - what is your biggest accomplishment and how long did it take to accomplish it? If you have a major accomplishment that took you over THREE YEARS - welcome to the club.

POS material

There are thousands of dollars worth of point of sale material in every sales office that goes unused. POS material is an excellent tool to get a person's attention. A big mistake is to give in to the overwhelming urge to talk while the customer is reading. Give the customer the sales brochure and be silent. Soon the customer will make a comment or ask a question. At that point you have succeeded in getting their attention.

Try an experiment the next time you call on a customer. Take a manila folder and write the persons name on the tab large enough so it can be easily read from across the desk. Put everything in the file you want to talk about and watch the reaction when you pull the file out and lay it on the table. The message you are sending is that you think this person is important enough to have a special file and you took the time to put together the items you wanted to talk about.

Another approach is to take your monthly flier and highlight the items each particular customer buys from you. This extra time will double the power of your fliers. Write their name on the POS before you go into the presentation and watch the difference.

Using samples

Another example is the use of samples. When a sample is given to a customer, we have the urge to tell them everything about it. The longer you can remain silent the more attention the customer will give to the sample. They have to be given a chance to look it over, taste it, feel it and smell it. We know so much about the product that we want to talk about it. The "Cutting Edge" salesperson will relax and give the customer some room to get involved with the sample. When it is time to talk, list the benefits of the product and watch for a positive reaction.

A small gift

Just about everyone in this country is in debt and just about everyone feels the responsibility to pay their debts. We can duplicate a strategy used for several years by a company that sold household products door to door. Their strategy was to knock on the door and when the prospect answered the salesperson would present them with a small gift. Because of our feeling of obligation to repay our debts, the prospect would listen to the sales presentation. The same feeling of obligation lies within every person we deal with. They may or may not repay the debt, nevertheless, they feel the obligation. The next time you make a cold call on a prospect, take along a small gift and present it at the beginning of the interview. It can be as simple as a company calendar, an ink pen or a note pad. Nine out of ten times they will repay you by listening to your presentation.

Industry news

Ever wonder why newspapers sell, why the evening news is one of the most watched programs on TV and why people subscribe to so many news feeds on their computer?

The answer to all these questions is the same. Do you think you know what it is?

The reason people come back to the news, and newspapers, is because of the word that's buried in both of these items -- "new."

That's the one thing everyone's interested in -- what's new. They want to know what's happening now, who's doing what, and why. They want to know what's unusual about it, what's odd about it, and if it affects them in any way.

You can win immediate attention by giving the prospect a piece of news about his or her business. It keeps the small talk "business-focused" so you're showing the customer that you are not there to waste time. Most importantly, the customer will have some genuine interest in it. And best of all, it shows that you know something about the industry and that you might very well be able to help provide a useful solution.

Most people spend very little time reading or studying about what's going on in their business. Much of the information comes from within their own company and it is often limited.

As a salesperson, the opportunity to gather facts, news and information is almost unlimited. In addition to all the trade journals you are exposed to you also have firsthand information from all the customers you call on and the many sales meetings you attend.

If you make your sales call "newsworthy", you'll be on your way to making the sale. Remember, people don't want to know what used to work, they want to know what works NOW. They want to know they're ahead of everyone else by using the latest breakthroughs and newest gadgets and achieving solutions as rapidly as possible.

You should be like a Crime Scene Investigator looking for newsworthy topics to bring to your customers. Not gossip, but industry trends, special reports, new ideas, success stories as well as stories of failure in the right context (helping them avoid the same mistakes).

As a resource for your customer your sales call should be anticipated by your customer because you help them stay up to date. As a salesperson you have the opportunity to be out in your market working, watching, listening and gathering information every day. Pass along useful information and you will always be welcome.

Always draw the line between sharing news and spreading gossip and you will always be respected. Spreading news does not mean that you should spread gossip or talk about other people's private business. It means bringing information that may be helpful to their business. Customers always appreciate copies of helpful information and it is well worth the effort it takes to find it and pass it along.

Keep that in mind next time you're trying to figure out how to attract your prospect's attention.

Your mental picture

The mental picture you have of your customer before you walk through the door will greatly affect the response you get.

Step aside and take a look at yourself as you get out of your car prior to calling on this person we shall assume is a stranger. As you walk into the warehouse, or step into the office, your attitude will be tremendously influenced by the planning you have done before you made this call. Are you carefully prepared and organized? This is a greater confidence builder than you realize.

How strong is the inner fire of belief in what you can do for him or her? Belief in your job is reflected the moment the customer looks at you.

Is your presentation logically arranged, with all data in order, so that you can automatically put your finger on any bit of evidence?

Have you figured out in advance exactly WHAT you are going to sell... perhaps, have written the order ready for his or her signature before you go in? There's nothing like such a concrete objective to help steer your course straight from your opening to your close.

Let's take a typical case. It's Monday morning. Your prospect has spent all day Sunday looking at new automobiles and expects to buy one this week. He came in late and is two hours behind with his work. He is getting ready for a conference call. He has an appointment at eleven thirty and had placed his watch on his desk to remind him. His wife has phoned and asked him to pay the mortgage at noon. He has just interviewed three people for a job opening. His mind is a million miles away from what you have to sell. In a fraction of a second you have got to clear his mind of a thousand disturbing thoughts which are crowding into his consciousness demanding attention. The moment he lays his eyes on you, his first reaction is one of self-protection! How can he get rid of you and get back to his automobile, his bills, and the routine of the day? Yet nearly everything he buys has been sold to him by salespeople who have known how to "cut through" that attitude and get attention.

What is your mental picture of this customer or prospect? Do you feel he or she is your superior and that you are liable to be a little embarrassed in their presence?

Get this mental picture right in your mind before making the call and the results will speak for themselves. Don't assume they are going to be eager to see you come through the door - be prepared.

Be mentally prepared! Just because they are not going to be eager to see you does not mean that you can't be eager to see them. It's all in your mind.

What if you received word that you inherited $500,000 just moments before you were going to see this person? Would you act more positive? Would you be excited? YES! You would probably make the sale without a hitch.

Then, after your appointment, you found out it was a mistake and you only inherited $500.

Don't wait for an inheritance - it's not coming.

Create demand

Create demand for your product or service.

When I lived in Orlando, Florida, the visionary Walt Disney had a team of folks buy all the property he needed to build Disney World. They were able to keep everyone sworn to secrecy. As soon as the purchase became known and everyone found out what was going on, the property values went sky high.

If you wanted to sell hot dogs in New York City you would have to buy a license. There are only a certain number of licenses available, which makes them increase in value. The current selling price for a hot dog cart license in New York City is between $350,000 and $500,000.

The same is true for a taxicab license.

The Los Angles Country Club was built in the 1950's at which time you could buy one of a thousand available memberships for $5,000. The standing price today is one million dollars.

You can see that people want what they can't have. When they can't have it, value is created.

How can this help you?

Here is an example.

There is a Martial Arts company near my home and my nephew is a member. When he first started going, he was getting a lot of individual attention. Being a member of the team was important. After one-year things started to change. The instructor wanted to go form 50 students to 150 students. He moved to a more expensive location, hired some help, and now spends most of his time chasing after new recruits to help pay for his increased overhead. He is actually making less money than he was with his original 50, many whom have left.

What if he understood the concept of supply and demand?

What if he would have raised his price and limited his students to 50. The only way you could become a member would be by referral and then you had to fill out an application and go through an interview process along with the parents. Interviews would be held only once per month on the second Tuesday from noon until 9:00 PM, by appointment.

What if, rather than answer his phone you heard a recording that said he was training his students and is unable to come to the phone because he didn't want to interrupt their focus and concentration.

What if all phone calls were returned at the end of the day by his wife (who works with him as his assistant) and finds out what they wanted. If it was important enough, a phone appointment would be set up with the instructor.

This is the same strategy doctors and dentists use to create a sense of being busy. They schedule appointment times close together and make you wait.

During your initial contact with a prospect, imply that you are only there to see if they qualify for you to spend time and energy helping them solve their problems.

Here is another example.

Trade show attendance has always a problem with many companies. Some of the smart companies are only allowing people to attend who are purchasing a certain dollar volume from them. They have even required an RSVP with a deposit that is refundable towards the purchase of anything at the show.

This is the law of supply and demand. If there is an unlimited supply, you and your products become a commodity. However, if you can somehow limit the supply, the demand will not only increase, the value will go up as well.

Attention: Get attention with an irresistible offer

Every time I visit a customer, I bring them something that will really help their business. It could be a very special price on an item, a piece of industry news, an idea that will help their business, something that will give them a competitive advantage, or perhaps something personal that I knew they were interested in. On every visit my customer says "wow, I really appreciate that!" I never make a call on a customer that is boring or routine. When they see me coming, they are sincerely excited to see me because I break the routine of their business by bringing value every time I make a sales call.

My 4% improvement objective:

_____

_____

_____

_____

_____

_____

What the entire book series will do for you

Buying all 13 books is like buying a library of 13 powerful coaching sessions that will increase every skill necessary for generating business. Once you experience the seemingly effortless improvement you will understand why there is a picture of Ben Franklin on every 100-dollar bill.

You will learn how to improve relationships, improve management skills, be more productive, generate more customers, negotiate better contracts, open new accounts, earn more profits and create more sales! Results most people only dream about! If you are a sales professional or an entrepreneur this is the perfect program to boost your sales and increase your profits.

Ben Franklin's system

In our fast-paced business and personal life today it has become increasingly difficult to set aside time for self development and improving your skills. With every spare minute taken up by reading blogs, logging on to Facebook, following people on Twitter, responding to text messages and emails and constantly talking on your cell phone, there seems to be little, if any, time left for learning new skills. Even the quiet time behind the wheel of your car is no longer available with satellite radio and cell phone coverage in every corner of the country.

Even though this seems like a new problem, distractions have been around forever. Two hundred years ago a man by the name of Ben Franklin had the same problem. He concluded that it was not a matter of distractions as much as a matter of focus. He set out to solve the problem and created the most effective system for self improvement ever invented.

Ben Franklin gives credit for all his success and accomplishments to the implementation of this system for the success he sought after. Despite being born into a poor family and only receiving two years of formal schooling, Ben Franklin became a successful printer, scientist, musician, author and one of the founding fathers of the United States. Ben Franklin is considered to have been one of the most persuasive and successful people in the history of the United States. He was a very skilled salesperson, marketer, negotiator and copywriter. Skills that every business owner, professional person, manager and marketer should have.

In the year 1723, Ben Franklin, at the age of seventeen, arrived in Philadelphia without a penny to his name. At age 42, he retired, wealthy, the first self made millionaire in the country. Few people, before or since have ever been as successful as Benjamin Franklin. He gave credit for his many inventions and business successes to his system for self improvement he created when he was 20 years old.

The key to Franklin's success was his drive to constantly improve himself and accomplish his ambitions. In order to accomplish his goal, Franklin developed and committed himself to a personal improvement program that consisted of mastering 13 principles.

When he was seventy-nine years old, Benjamin Franklin wrote more about this idea than anything else that ever happened to him in his entire life. He felt that he owed all his success and happiness to this one thing. Franklin wrote: "I hope, therefore, that some of my descendants may follow the example and reap the benefit."

Since success is developed by performing small and seemingly insignificant acts, you can use this method by reading and putting into practice the 13 skills that will guarantee your success in sales with scientific certainty.

This program takes advantage of Franklin's system and applies it to improving your skills as a sales professional. This program will show you how to dominate your market by first dominating yourself. By focusing on the 13 skills that make up a highly effective and successful sales professional. As these skills are improved your results and sales increases will also show a dramatic improvement.

The goal of going through the program the first time is to increase each skill by only four percent. With the accomplishment of this small improvement in each skill or attitude your overall improvement will be 52%. Those are results most people only dream about. However, you can accomplish this by investing as little as 45 minutes once a week reading one book and then focusing on improving the single skill during the rest of the week. The second week by reading the second book and focusing on that single skill during the week and so on until all 13 weeks are completed.

You can write the single word on the back of your business card and tape it to your dashboard as a reminder. You can put this one word on your smart phone as a reminder as well as on your email signature, your Facebook page or you can even have something worthwhile to tweet about. One word, one week, one skill, one "I am" statement, 4% improvement objective and your subconscious mind will receive the message through all the clutter and act on it.

After the first time through the process you can do as Ben Franklin suggests and go through the program a second, third and fourth time. Get your whole sales team on the same page at the same time and you will experience a whirlwind of new excitement and new business. Or get a like minded colleague and join forces with accountability and focus.

Achieve a 52% improvement

Using Franklin's scientific program for learning your objective is to improve 4% in each area over 13 weeks.

1. Attitude - Define what you want and go after it.
2. Respect - Earn respect-no more comfort zone.
3. Service - Help customers build their business.
4. Urgency - Be enthusiastic get things done now.
5. Confidence - Remove restrictions and limitations.
6. Persistence - Keep going and never give up.
7. Planning - Get big results by setting big goals.
8. Questions - Ask questions that make the sale.
9. Attention - Get attention with irresistible offers.
10. Presenting- Give reasons why they should buy.
11. Objections - Remove every roadblock to the sale.
12. Closing - Ask for the order and get paid.
13. Follow up - Remove all hope for competitors.

About the author Bob Oros (BobOros.com),

Bob Oros has been a full time speaker and author since 1992 with over 2,000 speaking engagements in all 50 states and several international locations as well as the author of 21 books on sales. Prior to starting his speaking career, Bob served six years in the US Navy as a Communications Specialist and then worked his way from a street sales person to the position of National Sales Manager for a Fortune 200 company.

CSP Award: Bob was awarded the designation of Certified Speaking Professional (CSP) by the National Speakers Association and the International Federation for Professional Speakers. Fewer than 10% of all speakers worldwide qualify for this award.

PWA Member: Bob is a member of the Professional Writers Alliance.

www.ingramcontent.com/pod-product-compliance
Lightning Source LLC
Chambersburg PA
CBHW070432180526
45158CB00017B/979